Picture Sequencing

Grades K-1

by
Helene Chirinian

Cover Art by
Ed Salmon

Frank Schaffer Publications®

Author: Helene Chirinian
Cover Artist: Ed Salmon

Frank Schaffer Publications®

Send all inquiries to:
Frank Schaffer Publications
8720 Orion Place
Columbus, Ohio 43240

Picture Sequencing—grades K–1

ISBN: 0-7682-0580-8

7 8 9 10 SNC 10 09

Name _____

What Comes Next?

Cut out the boxes at the bottom of the page. Paste them in the right places.

FS-8471 Picture Sequencing

What Comes Next?

Cut out the boxes at the bottom of the page. Paste them in the right places.

Name _____

What Comes Next?

Cut out the boxes at the bottom of the page. Paste them in the right places.

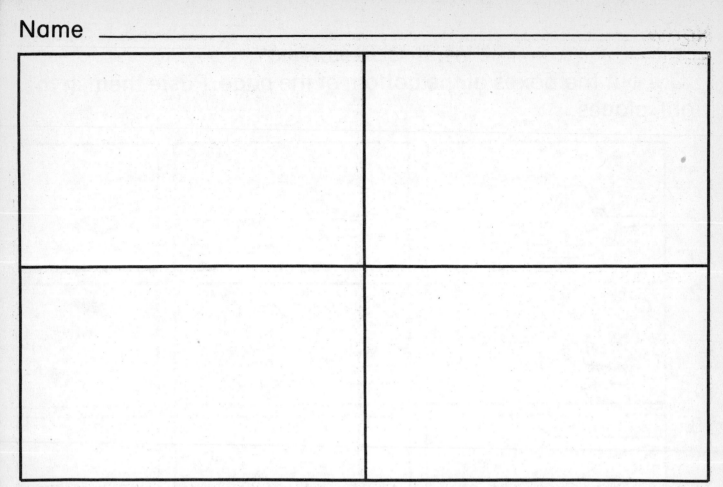

Cut out the pictures. Paste them in order above.

4

Name _____

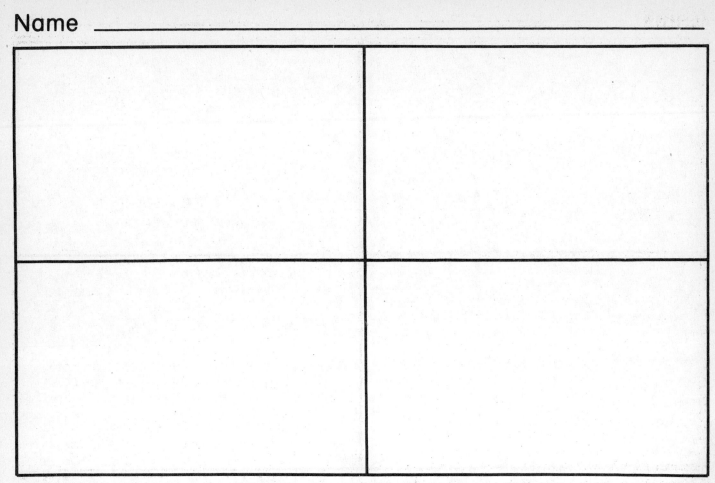

Cut out the pictures. Paste them in order above.

BOOK
CHECK·OUT

FS-8471 Picture Sequencing

Name _____

<table>
<tr><td></td><td></td></tr>
<tr><td></td><td></td></tr>
</table>

Cut out the pictures. Paste them in order above.

FS-8471 Picture Sequencing

Name _____

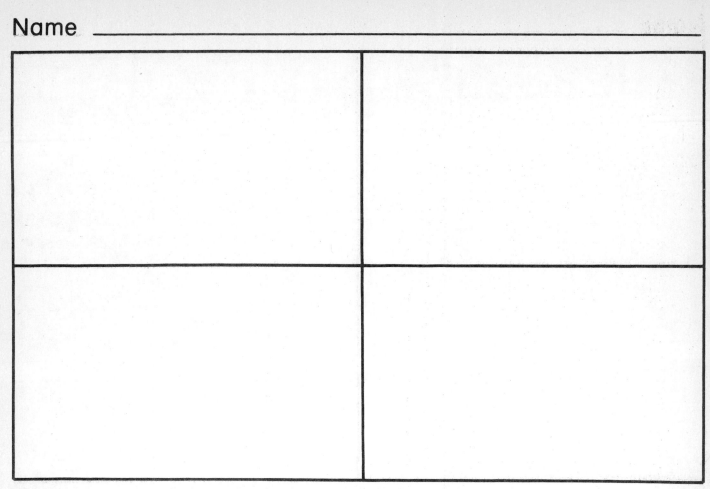

Cut out the pictures. Paste them in order above.

FS-8471 Picture Sequencing

Name _____

Cut out the pictures. Paste them in order above.

Cut out the pictures. Paste them in order above.

FS-8471 Picture Sequencing

Cut out the pictures. Paste them in order above.

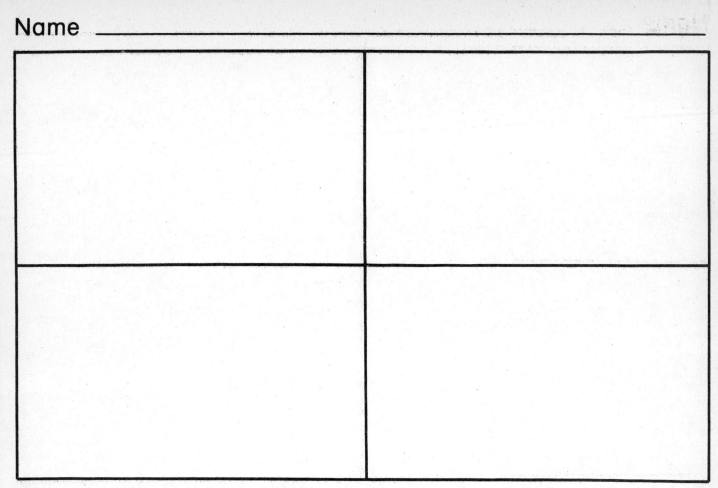

Cut out the pictures. Paste them in order above.

Cut out the pictures. Paste them in order above.

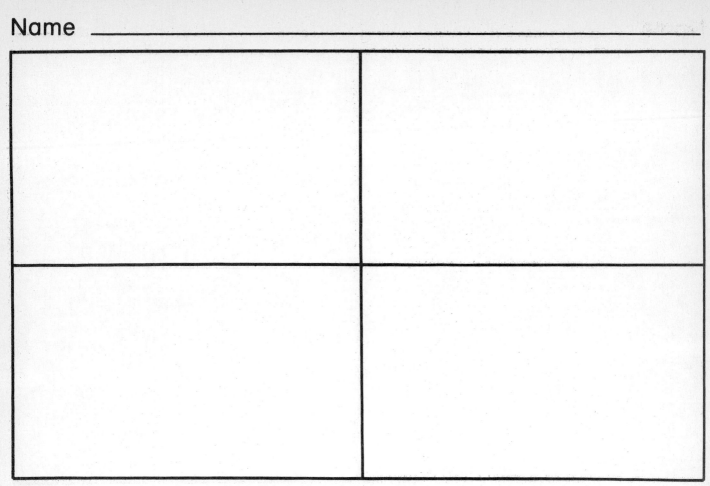

Cut out the pictures. Paste them in order above.

FS-8471 Picture Sequencing

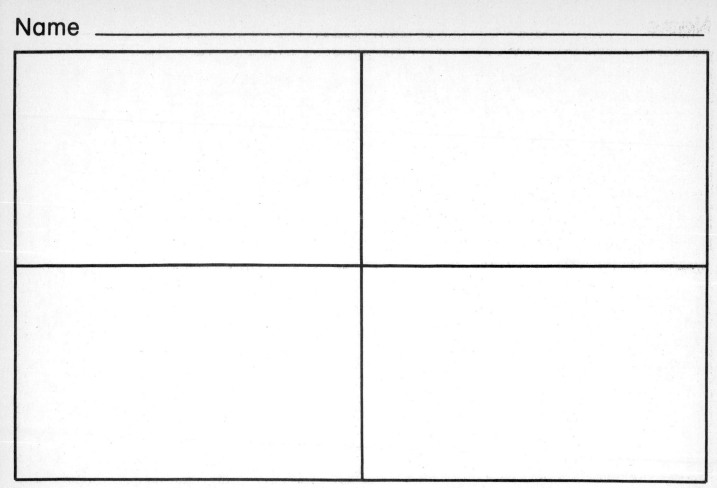

Cut out the pictures. Paste them in order above.

Name _____

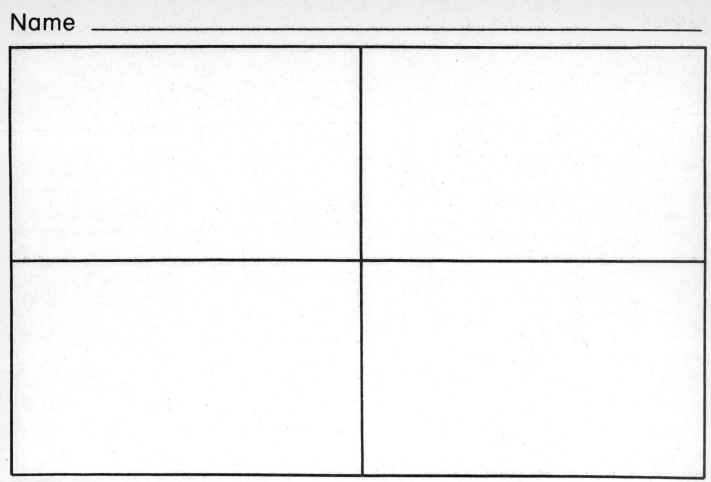

Cut out the pictures. Paste them in order above.

Name _____

Cut out the pictures. Paste them in order above.

FS-8471 Picture Sequencing

Name _____

Cut out the pictures. Paste them in order above.

FS-8471 Picture Sequencing

Name _____

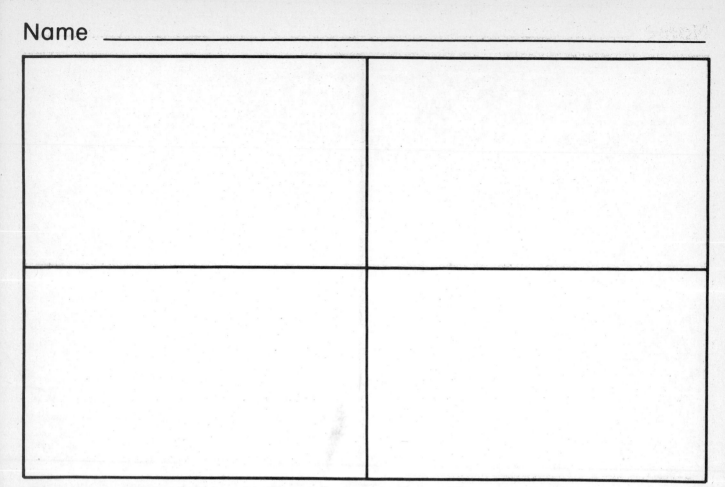

Cut out the pictures. Paste them in order above.

18

Name _____

Cut out the pictures. Paste them in order above.

_____

Cut out the pictures. Paste them in order above.